MW00898412

THIS JOURNAL
BELONGS TO

....

....

Made in the USA
Monee, IL
20 June 2022

98319639R00069